Original title:
The Symphony of Support

Copyright © 2024 Swan Charm
All rights reserved.

Author: Johan Kirsipuu
ISBN HARDBACK: 978-9916-86-581-1
ISBN PAPERBACK: 978-9916-86-582-8
ISBN EBOOK: 978-9916-86-583-5

Whispers of Hope

In the dawn's gentle light,
Dreams take their flight,
Whispers of hope call,
Chasing shadows of night.

In the stillness, we breathe,
Promises we weave,
Hearts open wide,
To the love we believe.

Through the storms that may rise,
We find strength in the ties,
Holding on to each other,
Under vast, endless skies.

With each step we take,
A new path we make,
Guided by the stars,
No fear of the ache.

Hope flows like a stream,
Carrying our dream,
In the whispers we share,
Together, we beam.

Resonance of Resilience

In the midst of the fight,
We stand, fierce and bright,
Resilience our armor,
Shining through the night.

With each challenge we face,
We find strength, embrace,
Echoes of courage rise,
In this sacred space.

When the world seems unjust,
In each other we trust,
Through valleys of sorrow,
We rise from the dust.

As seasons shift and change,
We'll adapt, rearrange,
In the dance of our lives,
We'll overcome the strange.

Resonance in our hearts,
Creating new starts,
Together, unbroken,
Resilience imparts.

A Tapestry of Trust

Woven threads intertwine,
Stories yours and mine,
A tapestry of trust,
In each gentle line.

Through laughter and tears,
We conquer our fears,
In the fabric of time,
Our bond perseveres.

In moments unchecked,
Love's warmth we respect,
Each thread tells a tale,
Of hearts we protect.

Brighter than the sun,
Together, we're one,
In the weave of our lives,
Trust cannot be undone.

A tapestry so rich,
In every stitch,
Bound by shared visions,
We find our true niche.

The Rhythm of Remembrance

In the silence, we pause,
Reflecting on the cause,
The rhythm of remembrance,
Echoes without flaws.

With every beat of time,
Our hearts start to rhyme,
Cherished voices linger,
In memory, they climb.

Stories softly spoken,
Connections unbroken,
In the dance of the past,
New futures are woven.

We hold close the days,
In countless arrays,
The rhythm of remembrance,
Guides us through the maze.

As we journey ahead,
With love, we are led,
In the rhythm of life,
We honor the dead.

Chords of Life

In the silence, whispers ring,
Echoes of the songs we sing.
Notes of joy, notes of strife,
Crafting the chords of life.

Melodies that rise and fall,
Binding hearts with every call.
Strumming strings both soft and bright,
Guiding us through day and night.

In the harmony we find,
Threads of love that intertwine.
A symphony both loud and clear,
Filling the soul with cheer.

Each chord played, a story told,
In the music, we grow bold.
From the shadows, we take flight,
Chasing dreams into the light.

Together in this vibrant sound,
Where our hopes and joys abound.
Life's sweet song will ever thrive,
In these endless chords, we strive.

Waves of Warmth

On the shore, the tides embrace,
Gentle waves, a softening grace.
Sun-kissed sands beneath our feet,
Where the land and ocean meet.

Ripples dance with salty foam,
Calling out to heart and home.
Each wave brings a soothing balm,
Nature's touch, a perfect calm.

Beneath the sky, so vast and blue,
We find peace in every hue.
Waves of warmth, a soft caress,
In this moment, we are blessed.

The sun sets low, a golden glow,
As evening whispers, tides will flow.
In the twilight, dreams arise,
Underneath the starlit skies.

Together we will ride the tide,
In its embrace, we will confide.
Waves of warmth around us pour,
We are home, forevermore.

Chiming in Unison

Bells that ring in morning light,
Calling forth the day so bright.
Chiming softly, side by side,
In harmony, we take pride.

Voices blend, a sweet refrain,
Lifting spirits, easing pain.
Like a chorus through the air,
In every heart, we find our share.

Melodies that twist and swirl,
Spirits dancing, dreams unfurl.
In the echoes, find our trace,
Singing together, a warm embrace.

Rhythms pulse like beating hearts,
Binding us when life departs.
In this song of love and trust,
We will rise, we will adjust.

Chiming in unison we sway,
Coloring the world today.
In this symphony of ours,
We bloom like vibrant flowers.

Embraces in Euphony

In the twilight, shadows play,
Softly woven words we say.
Embraces found in every note,
In harmony, our hearts will float.

Melodic whispers fill the air,
Anointing dreams with gentle care.
Lifting spirits, weaving love,
Like the stars that shine above.

Resonating deep within,
In each chord, new lives begin.
Singing softly, hand in hand,
In this euphony, we stand.

Every heartbeat, every sigh,
Carries tales of days gone by.
Lost in music, found in grace,
Together in this sacred space.

Embraces in this sweet refrain,
Washing over like gentle rain.
In the echoes of our song,
Together is where we belong.

Pulse of Partnership

In every heartbeat's thrill,
We weave our dreams anew,
Two minds as one, we climb,
Together, we break through.

With trust that binds us tight,
We spark a vibrant flame,
Through trials and through joys,
In unity, we claim.

Each voice a vital note,
In harmony, we stand,
Our pulse a force of change,
With courage, we expand.

The strength we share is vast,
In partnership, we rise,
With hope our guiding star,
Together, we'll touch skies.

So let our spirits dance,
In rhythm, hand in hand,
Building bridges of light,
In this vast, wondrous land.

Ensemble of Empowerment

Voices blend and soar,
A symphony of grace,
In unity, we find,
Our rightful, equal place.

Each story shared ignites,
A fire deep within,
With courage, we will rise,
And let the journey begin.

Empowered hearts unite,
We stand in pure delight,
With dreams held high and bright,
Together, we take flight.

No challenge is too great,
When we all lift each other,
In this grand ensemble,
We strengthen one another.

So hear the call of change,
With every note we play,
An anthem of our strength,
Together, we will stay.

Melody of Mentorship

In gentle guiding hands,
New paths begin to form,
With wisdom shared like light,
We break the darkest storm.

A melody so sweet,
Of lessons learned and taught,
In every note we share,
A bond that can't be bought.

Together we explore,
Embracing all the flaws,
With patience as our guide,
We'll thrive without a pause.

Through laughter and through tears,
Our journeys intertwine,
In this great dance of growth,
Our spirits brightly shine.

So let the music flow,
In harmony, we stride,
The melody of hope,
In mentorship, our pride.

Crescendo of Community

We gather as one voice,
In celebration's bright glow,
Together, we will stand,
In love, our spirits grow.

Each story we embrace,
A thread in shared design,
In diversity, we bloom,
Creating ties that bind.

Through laughter and through care,
Our hearts beat in the same,
With kindness as our song,
We'll weave a lasting name.

As challenges arise,
We'll face them hand in hand,
In unity, we'll spark,
A light across the land.

So let us lift each other,
In every voice, a key,
Our crescendo of community,
A vibrant tapestry.

The Harmony of Healing

In whispers soft, the night begins,
Where gentle hearts can heal their sins.
A touch, a word, a glance anew,
Bringing peace in shades of blue.

With every breath, we learn to feel,
The silent strength in wounds that heal.
In shared silence, our fears dissolve,
Together we find what's lost, evolve.

The laughter shared beneath the moon,
Embraces pain and brings a tune.
With open arms, we learn to sway,
In harmony, we greet the day.

Through vibrant dreams, we weave our thread,
Of love and hope that lies ahead.
In unity, our spirits rise,
To dance beneath the starlit skies.

So let us tread on paths unknown,
In search of kindness, seeds we've sown.
For in this journey, hand in hand,
We build our world, a healing land.

The Blend of Belief

In colors bright, our hopes combine,
Each thread a story, yours and mine.
Through woven tales, our spirits soar,
Uniting hearts forevermore.

As rivers flow, diverse yet one,
In every heart, the spark of sun.
Together in our quest for truth,
We share the wisdom of our youth.

With faith as strong as ancient trees,
We stand for love, for peace, for ease.
Through trials faced and joys embraced,
In every moment, hope is chased.

In whispered prayers beneath the sky,
Our voices blend; they rise, they fly.
With hands outstretched toward the light,
We build a future, brave and bright.

So let the world see our embrace,
In every creed, in every space.
For in this blend, our dreams ignite,
Together we shine, a guiding light.

Together We Thrive

With every step, we find our way,
In unity, we seize the day.
Through obstacles, we rise and grow,
In every heart, a fire's glow.

Friends by our side, we dare to dream,
In laughter's light, we form a team.
With kindness shared and burdens light,
We stand together, strong in might.

Through storms that come, we learn to dance,
In courage found, we take a chance.
Each moment shared, a treasure new,
In harmony, our spirits grew.

With every challenge, hand in hand,
We forge a bond, a promised land.
In every triumph, love will guide,
Together we stand, side by side.

So let the world see what we've built,
In every laugh, in every quilt.
For as we thrive, our hearts align,
In shared adventure, your hand in mine.

Supportive Serenades

In gentle chords, our voices blend,
A melody that will not end.
Through trials faced, we sing and soar,
In harmony, we are much more.

With dulcet tones, we lift our tears,
In every note, we chase our fears.
With every strum, we weave our dreams,
Together finding all that gleams.

As seasons change, our rhythms shift,
In every heart, a precious gift.
Through ups and downs, we tune our song,
In unity, we all belong.

As evening falls, the stars appear,
In whispered notes, we draw them near.
With every lyric softly sung,
We find the joy from which we sprung.

So let our voices rise in cheer,
For in each other, we draw near.
Through supportive serenades we find,
A bond eternal, heart and mind.

Crescendo of Courage

In shadows deep, the voice will rise,
With hearts ignited, we'll touch the skies.
Each step we take, a bold decree,
Together strong, we'll break the free.

The whispers doubt, yet still we stand,
With hope ablaze, we hold the hand.
Through trials faced, we learn to roar,
Emboldened spirits, we seek for more.

In every heart, a journey flows,
With strength to share, our courage grows.
We push the limits, face the pain,
In unity, the light will remain.

Mountains high, we'll climb as one,
With dreams alight, we've just begun.
In every heartbeat, courage sings,
The world awaits what daring brings.

Unison of Understanding

In silent moments, wisdom speaks,
With open hearts, connection peaks.
We gather close, through eyes we see,
A tapestry of harmony.

Words may differ, yet thoughts align,
In shared embrace, our souls combine.
Through listening, we start to know,
A bridge is built where kindness flows.

Together we frame the world anew,
In shades of empathy, bright and true.
With every story shared, we pave,
A path of grace, our hearts to save.

The dance of minds, a tender waltz,
With every step, we find no faults.
In unison, we rise and stand,
United dreams, a guiding hand.

The Key to Empathy

An open door, a gentle space,
Where kindness blooms, and hearts embrace.
We seek to find what lies within,
A life mirrored, where love begins.

In every tear, a tale is spun,
With threads of grace, where all are one.
The key we hold, a simple glance,
To walk together in this dance.

With open ears, we listen clear,
To whispers soft, and shadows near.
In understanding, we bridge the gap,
Creating bonds, a heartfelt map.

Beneath our skin, the stories flow,
With every heartbeat, we come to know.
The key to hearts, a sacred trust,
To nurture love, to rise from dust.

Interludes of Inspiration

In fleeting moments, sparks ignite,
With thoughts that soar, like birds in flight.
A breath of hope, a dash of grace,
In every heart, we find our place.

The canvas wide, our dreams unfurl,
In colors bright, we paint the world.
With whispers soft, our minds take flight,
Inspiration dances in the light.

When storms may rage, and shadows loom,
We find our voice, dispelling gloom.
With every heartache, seeds we sow,
Of wisdom's touch, we'll surely grow.

So, let us share the tales we weave,
In every word, a chance to believe.
Through interludes of joy and pain,
Inspiration's fire shall remain.

Chords of Compassion

In the quiet of the night,
Hearts beat soft and slow,
Tender whispers fill the air,
Kindness starts to glow.

A hand upon a shoulder,
Lifts the weight of pain,
Together we find solace,
In sunshine and in rain.

Each story gently woven,
Into a tapestry,
We share our hopes and dreams,
Beneath the timeless tree.

The chords of love are ringing,
In harmony we stand,
Bridges built through courage,
United hand in hand.

Compassion is our music,
In every note we raise,
With hearts that beat as one,
We find our strength to praise.

Cadence of Caring

In the rhythm of our days,
We find our gentle song,
A melody of friendship,
Where all of us belong.

With every step we take,
A dance of hearts so true,
In the cadence of our caring,
We lift each other too.

Through trials and through triumphs,
We celebrate the now,
Each laugh becomes a heartbeat,
Each tear a shared vow.

Our voices blend together,
In harmony and peace,
As we weave the fabric,
Of love that will not cease.

In this rhythm of our lives,
Compassion is the key,
With every note of kindness,
We set each other free.

Orchestration of Togetherness

In a world that spins so fast,
We find our steady beat,
Like a symphony of voices,
Our hearts in time repeat.

Each note a shared connection,
In life's grand, swirling dance,
We create a landscape vibrant,
Through chance and by romance.

With every heartbeat shared,
We compose a timeless piece,
From laughter and from heartache,
Our melodies increase.

In the orchestration of hope,
We let our spirits soar,
With every chord of kindness,
We open every door.

Together, we are stronger,
A symphony so bright,
In the concert of our lives,
We shine, a beacon light.

The Sound of Solidarity

In the echoes of our voices,
We find the strength to stand,
Each sound a note of courage,
United in this band.

Through storms that may assail us,
We hold each other tight,
For in the sound of solidarity,
We find our shared light.

With every challenge faced,
Comes the chance to unite,
In the chorus of our stories,
We rise to greet the night.

Together in the struggle,
We elevate our song,
Building bridges strong and true,
Where every heart belongs.

The sound of hope is ringing,
Through valleys deep and wide,
In solidarity, we'll flourish,
Together, side by side.

Vibrations of Vitality

In the morning light, we wake,
Nature's pulse, the earth's heartbeats.
Every breath, a spark ignites,
Life's rhythm, a dance so sweet.

Colors bloom, the world ignites,
Joyful sounds fill every space.
In the silence, whispers stir,
Vibrations of our vibrant grace.

Each moment sings a bright refrain,
Hope flows through our open veins.
The essence of our being thrives,
In unity, our spirit gains.

Let laughter rise, let kindness soar,
In every heart, let love abide.
Together we shall weave the thread,
Of vibrant life that won't subside.

So when the night begins to fall,
Remember joy shall light the way.
Vibrations of vitality,
Will guide us through each passing day.

The Dance of Dependence

In the shadows, we rely,
Upon each other's gentle hands.
Support is found in every sigh,
In trust, our unity withstands.

Together we weave our needs,
Through tangled paths we gently tread.
In sharing burdens, heartache leads,
To the blooms of love unsaid.

A dance unfolds, we take our turns,
In harmony, we learn to sway.
As ebb and flow with life discern,
We grow together, day by day.

Each heartbeat echoes in the night,
A symphony of souls entwined.
In dependence, we find our light,
Our strengths reflected, hearts aligned.

So take my hand, let's spin around,
In this dance, our stories blend.
Through every step, in joy we've found,
The beauty of our shared depend.

The Sound of Belonging

In gentle whispers, love is shared,
A haven where our hearts reside.
In every laugh and every tear,
The bonds we build, our eternal guide.

The echo of our footsteps trace,
A path where kindness learns to grow.
In unison, we find our place,
The sound of belonging, soft and low.

Around the table, stories flow,
Embraces wrap us warm and tight.
In memories, the past will glow,
The sound of love, a pure delight.

Through trials faced and struggles shared,
In every challenge, we stand strong.
A melody, our spirits paired,
The sound of belonging, our sweet song.

So let the world around us fade,
In harmony, we shall remain.
For in this space, love is our trade,
The sound of belonging, our refrain.

Cantata of Connection

In the tapestry of time, we weave,
Moments stitched with golden thread.
Through laughter's grace, and hearts that cleave,
A cantata of connection spread.

The notes we sing, a vibrant tune,
In harmony, we find our way.
Underneath the watchful moon,
In unity, our spirits sway.

With every glance, we bridge the gap,
A dance of souls in whispered song.
Through every hug, we close the map,
Of distance that once felt so long.

In circles drawn, we join our hands,
As echoes of our dreams collide.
In understanding, love expands,
A cantata of connection, our guide.

So let us lift our voices high,
In symphony, we will ascend.
Together we shall touch the sky,
In this cantata, love won't end.

Acoustic Allies

In the quiet nights we share,
Soft whispers drift in the air.
Guitars strum, hearts align,
Together we make the stars shine.

Melodies harmonize our souls,
Bridging gaps, making us whole.
With every note, bonds grow tight,
In the stillness, pure delight.

Underneath the moon's soft glare,
Every song shows how we care.
Together in this rhythmic flow,
Our spirits rise, our dreams glow.

We dance to tunes both old and new,
In this moment, just me and you.
With laughter, joy, and gentle strife,
Music maps the path of life.

These acoustic allies, side by side,
With every chord, we take the ride.
In this symphony, we belong,
Forever united in our song.

Bridges of Belonging

Across the chasms wide and deep,
We build connections, ours to keep.
Each step we take, hand in hand,
Creating bridges in this land.

With voices raised, we pave the way,
To light the dark, to break the gray.
Through laughter shared and tears we've shed,
In every moment, love is bred.

Hearts interwoven, strong and true,
Together facing each day anew.
With open arms, we make a stand,
Finding strength in this band.

In unity we find our power,
With every hug, in every hour.
These bridges span the voids we face,
In the warmth of our embrace.

Through trials faced and dreams pursued,
We nurture hope and gratitude.
In this tapestry of grace,
We forge our paths, a bright embrace.

Serenade of Strength

In the dark, your voice I hear,
A gentle song that draws me near.
With courage wrapped in every line,
A serenade of strength divine.

Through shadows cast, you light the way,
With every note, keep doubts at bay.
In whispered verses, love ignites,
Empowering us to reach new heights.

Together facing storms that rage,
We turn each page, we break the cage.
With melodies that lift our dreams,
In harmony, we find our themes.

These trials shape the hearts we hold,
In every setback, courage bold.
Our song, a testament of might,
In the darkest times, we shine bright.

With every beat, we rise, we strive,
This serenade keeps hopes alive.
In the echo of our fight,
We find our strength, our guiding light.

Waves of Warmth

Feel the tide, the ocean's pull,
In its rhythm, hearts are full.
Waves of warmth crash on the shore,
Bringing love, forevermore.

Beneath the sun's embrace we play,
As laughter dances in the spray.
With every splash, we share a dream,
Together, a vibrant team.

As stars awaken in the sky,
We watch the currents glide and sigh.
In this calm, our spirits blend,
In the waves, love has no end.

With every ripple, hope we cast,
Creating memories that will last.
These waves of warmth, a gentle song,
In unity, we all belong.

Together we stand, shore to shore,
In the sea of life, we explore.
With open hearts, we sail the sea,
Waves of warmth, just you and me.

Harmonized Hearts

In the melody of every sigh,
Our spirits dance and intertwine.
Together we rise, we touch the sky,
In this bond, our love will shine.

Every heartbeat plays a tune,
A rhythm soft, a sweet refrain.
Underneath the silver moon,
Together we withstand the strain.

In harmony, our dreams align,
Notes of trust and longing blend.
As seasons change, our love will twine,
A symphony that knows no end.

Through the storms and gentle breeze,
Our hearts beat in perfect time.
With every whisper, we find ease,
Creating life, a love sublime.

Together, we are never lost,
A melody that won't betray.
In every joy, we share the cost,
In our hearts, the music stays.

Mutual Melodies

In every note, a story told,
Two souls blend, a sacred trust.
With each refrain, we break the mold,
Creating harmony, a must.

Your laughter dances in the air,
A sweet serenade in the night.
In mutual love, we both care,
Striking chords that feel so right.

Through whispered dreams and shared delight,
We compose an endless song.
Hand in hand, we chase the light,
In this bond, we both belong.

With every challenge, we will rise,
A duet strong, an echo clear.
Together facing any guise,
In mutual trust, we persevere.

As time flows like a gentle stream,
We'll nurture this fluid art.
With every breath, we'll dream our dream,
In mutual melodies, we'll part.

Links of Loyalty

In quiet strength, our promises lie,
Bound by trust, both near and far.
Through shared glances, we never say goodbye,
Our bonds like constellations, a guiding star.

With every step, we walk as one,
In laughter bright and silence deep.
Through endless battles, we've already won,
In loyalty, our hearts will keep.

Through storms that rage and skies of gray,
Our links of loyalty won't break.
Together we shine, come what may,
In unity, we're wide awake.

In secret whispers, we find our way,
With woven threads that never fray.
Through trials faced, we proudly stay,
As loyal hearts in light of day.

Life's tapestry we weave so fine,
With love's refrain, we stay the course.
In every struggle, you are mine,
Our loyalty, a powerful force.

Confidence in Consonance

In every syllable, strength is found,
A chorus bold, our voices blend.
In consonance, we stand our ground,
Together facing what life sends.

With every word, a promise made,
Our spirits lift, unbroken trust.
In perfect harmony, unafraid,
In this union, love is just.

With shared goals and dreams in sight,
We forge our path through thick and thin.
In confidence, we find our light,
Two hearts that resonate within.

Through trials faced and victories won,
Our love's a rhythm, a vital dance.
With every breath, we become one,
In consonance, we take our chance.

So let the world hear our sweet song,
In confidence, we rise and soar.
Together, right where we belong,
In consonance forevermore.

Interludes of Inspiration

Beneath the sky so wide and clear,
Dreams take flight without a fear.
Each thought a spark, igniting the night,
Guiding the heart towards the light.

Moments gathered like gentle rain,
Nurturing seeds through joy and pain.
Whispers of hopes in the breeze,
Carry us softly with such ease.

A canvas painted with shades of grace,
Every brushstroke finds its place.
Inspiration flows like a river,
Flowing fast, making hearts quiver.

Paths of purpose intertwine,
Leading each soul to the divine.
In the quiet, hearts align,
Finding strength in every sign.

Embrace the journey, cherish the ride,
With open arms, let love reside.
For in the dance of life's sweet song,
We find the place where we belong.

Aria of Assurance

In the melody of whispered dreams,
Confidence rises like sunlit beams.
Each note a promise softly sung,
Lifting spirits, forever young.

With every heartbeat comes the trust,
That in the journey, we are robust.
Voices echo in harmony sweet,
Guiding all souls with rhythmic feet.

A symphony of strength unifies,
With every challenge, hope never dies.
In the chorus of hearts held tight,
We become brave, embracing the fight.

As shadows fall, and dreams take flight,
We rise together, hearts alight.
With courage sewn into our seams,
We chase the glory of our dreams.

So let the world hear our refrain,
A song of love that breaks the chain.
With each refrain, let doubt disperse,
In this aria, our hearts converse.

Echoing Embraces

In the stillness, hearts collide,
Echoes of laughter far and wide.
Each embrace a moment shared,
In the silence, love is declared.

The warmth of presence, soft and near,
Whispers of hope that calm our fear.
In every touch, a story flows,
Binding souls where friendship grows.

As twilight descends, shadows play,
Memories rise, never to sway.
In the dance of time, we find grace,
Every heartbeat a sweet embrace.

Through valleys deep and mountains high,
Together we'll soar, reaching the sky.
In echoes resounding, let love lead,
In these moments, we are freed.

So gather 'round, let voices blend,
In this harmony, hearts will mend.
With every echo, let love remain,
Together we blossom, breaking the chain.

Whispers of Wisdom

In quiet moments, truths emerge,
Whispers of wisdom begin to surge.
Listen closely to nature's song,
Guiding us gently, where we belong.

Through storms and sun, the journey weaves,
Each lesson learned, a treasure retrieves.
In every challenge, strength is found,
Roots grow deep within the ground.

As shadows dance beneath the trees,
Ancient tales float on the breeze.
In the stillness, our hearts can see,
The threads of fate, in harmony.

With open minds, we seek to know,
The path unfolds, by faith we grow.
Embrace the shadows, cherish the light,
In the whispers, wisdom ignites.

So linger long in the soft embrace,
Of nature's voice, her knowing grace.
For in the stillness, truths reside,
Guiding our steps, the wise abide.

A Ballad of Benevolence

In a world where kindness grows,
Hearts entwined like vines,
Gentle whispers, soft and low,
In each act, a love that shines.

With open arms, we gather near,
Sharing burdens, lightening loads,
In the warm embrace of cheer,
Compassion flows, a river roads.

A simple smile, a hand to lend,
In the shadows, we find our light,
Together strong, we can amend,
In harmony, the stars ignite.

Through stormy days and quiet nights,
We weave our dreams, a tapestry,
With every thread, we share our sights,
Building hopes, just you and me.

So let us dance to love's sweet tune,
With hearts aligned, we rise above,
In every sun, in every moon,
A ballad sung of boundless love.

Flourishing in Harmony

Underneath the wide blue sky,
Where laughter blooms like flowers,
We spread our wings, we learn to fly,
Joined as one in nature's powers.

With every note of joy we find,
The symphony of life unfolds,
With hearts aligned, in every kind,
Together, dreams are freely told.

In gardens rich, where hope takes root,
We nurture peace in every heart,
Through every storm, we bear the fruit,
United, we shall never part.

Together, hand in hand we stand,
In rhythm with the earth's sweet song,
With trust and love, we firm our band,
A harmony, forever strong.

So let the winds of fate guide us,
In unity, we'll never part,
A chorus sung, in love we trust,
Flourishing, we each play our part.

Cadences of Comfort

When shadows creep and silence falls,
We find our strength in tender grace,
In quiet rooms, where heartbeats call,
We gather close, a warm embrace.

With whispered hopes and gentle care,
Through every trial, we shall stay,
In the soft hum of love we share,
We craft a light to guide our way.

Through rising tides and fading light,
Our bond shall always pull us near,
In sorrow's depths, there shines a bright,
A beacon of our trust and cheer.

Each smile exchanged, a thread of gold,
We stitch a quilt of memories,
In the arms of love, we unfold,
The warmth that truly sets us free.

So in the stillness, hear our song,
A melody of heart and soul,
In cadence, we will all belong,
For in comfort, we are whole.

The Ballad of Togetherness

In every heart, a story sleeps,
In shared moments, we find grace,
Through laughter bright and longing weeps,
Together, we embrace our space.

With steps entwined upon the path,
We tread with care where wildflowers bloom,
In unity, we dance through wrath,
Finding joy in every room.

Through stormy nights, when dreams grow dim,
Our voices rise in sweet refrain,
In harmony, we sing for him,
For her, for all, in joy and pain.

No matter where the journey leads,
We hold the hands that guide us through,
In every heart, the love that feeds,
Together bright, forever true.

So let us weave this tale of old,
In threads of laughter, love, and light,
The ballad of our hearts be told,
In togetherness, we shine so bright.

Ballad of Benevolence

In a village where kindness blooms,
Hearts entwined, dispelling glooms.
Hands reach out, a helping hand,
Together, we make our stand.

Whispers of love, a gentle breeze,
Among the trees, the laughter frees.
In every act, a spark ignites,
Illuminating darkest nights.

A stranger smiles, a bond is cast,
Echoes of joy, forever last.
In every tear, a story told,
In every heart, a light of gold.

Through trials faced, we learn, we grow,
In unity's strength, the truth shall flow.
Together we rise, hand in hand,
Benevolence, the heart's command.

With compassion wrapped in grace,
We find our way, we find our place.
A ballad sung, in harmony,
Forever bound in empathy.

Lyrics of Lifelines

In the fabric of life we weave,
Threads of hope, we dare believe.
Every voice a note, divine,
In the chorus, our hearts align.

Through storms and trials, we persist,
Waves of courage, we cannot resist.
Each whisper shared, a bond does rise,
In every tear, a promise lies.

Lifelines dance on the edge of fate,
Through laughter shared, we celebrate.
A melody soft, a guiding star,
Together, we'll venture far.

With dreams entwined, we chart the skies,
In every struggle, our spirit flies.
Holding hands, we brave the night,
In the lyrics of love, we find our light.

So let us sing, our voices blend,
In the symphony that will never end.
Each heartbeat a testament to time,
In life's vast rhythm, we all rhyme.

Unison of Understanding

In the silence where secrets dwell,
A heart speaks loud, a story to tell.
Understanding blooms in shared silence,
In empathy's embrace, we find balance.

With every glance, a language flows,
In the warmth shared, compassion grows.
No words are needed, just pure intent,
In the bond of trust, our spirits are lent.

We walk together, in step, side by side,
Through valleys low, and mountains wide.
In our journey, we learn to see,
The beauty in our diversity.

In shared laughter, a union is found,
In every heartbeat, a common sound.
With open hearts, we pave the way,
In understanding, we set hearts at bay.

So let us listen, and let us care,
In the unison of life we share.
Hand in hand, we'll break down the walls,
In the melody of life, love calls.

Tapestry of Trust

In threads of faith, we weave our dreams,
Bright and vibrant, like sunlit beams.
Embroidered with hope, our visions align,
In every stitch, a love that shines.

Trust is a fabric, strong yet fine,
Woven together, your hand in mine.
In each moment, we find our place,
A tapestry rich, with warmth and grace.

Through trials faced, we will prevail,
In unity, we will never pale.
A tapestry of colors bold,
In its embrace, our lives unfold.

With every pulse, the threads entwine,
In symphony, our hearts align.
Together we face the rising tide,
In the tapestry of trust, we abide.

So let us cherish, each woven part,
In the fabric of life, we play our part.
With trust as our guide, we journey on,
In the tapestry of love, we are never alone.

An Ode to Uplifting

In shadows deep, we find the light,
A gentle whisper, a soaring flight.
With every heart, a song we share,
In the warmth of love, we learn to care.

Together we rise, hand in hand,
In laughter's grace, together we stand.
The burdens lift, the spirits soar,
In unity's bond, we crave for more.

Through trials faced, the strength we gain,
Like flowers blooming after rain.
Each moment shines, a precious gift,
In the joy of living, our spirits lift.

A tapestry woven, rich and bright,
In every soul, a spark of light.
With kindness sown, our seeds are cast,
In love's embrace, we find our path.

So let us sing, and let us soar,
With open hearts, forevermore.
In uplifting waves, we find our way,
United we stand, come what may.

Village Voices

In the quiet of the evening glow,
The village whispers, soft and low.
Children laugh, their joy spills wide,
In their simple games, where dreams abide.

From door to door, the stories flow,
Of summer's sun and winter's snow.
Neighbors wave, with hearts so kind,
In every glance, true friendship find.

The market bustles, colors bright,
Old and young share in delight.
Fruits and flowers, fresh and fair,
Each basket holds the village's care.

At twilight's fall, the stars appear,
Voices blend, in joy and cheer.
Around the fire, tales are spun,
In the warm embrace, we are all one.

In every corner, the echoes play,
Of timeless love, in their own way.
The village hums its sweet refrain,
A melody of life, joy, and pain.

Blessed in the Echo

In the valleys where silence reigns,
The echoes whisper sweet refrains.
Nature's hum, a soothing sound,
In every heartbeat, life is found.

The mountains stand, their peaks so tall,
Holding stories, ancient and small.
As rivers flow, their tales unwind,
In every twist, new lessons find.

Leaves rustle soft in the gentle breeze,
A symphony sung among the trees.
With each step, the ground does speak,
In every pause, it softly peaks.

Moments linger, the past does glow,
In the blessings found in what we know.
The echo carries, a timeless grace,
In the sacred dance, we find our place.

So let us listen, hearts awake,
In every echo, a chance to take.
For life's sweet song is ours to share,
In the blessed echo, we are rare.

Collective Crescendo

From whispered thoughts, a chorus grows,
In every heart, a passion flows.
With voices raised, the dream takes flight,
A symphony born from dark to light.

Together we stand, a vibrant throng,
In unity's strength, we must belong.
Through each refrain, the spirit swells,
In harmony's embrace, a tale it tells.

The rhythms pulse, in every beat,
In shared resolve, we stand, complete.
With every note, a story shared,
In the finest moments, hearts are bared.

We dance through storms, we leap through fears,
In every triumph, through all the tears.
For in the struggle, our spirits shine,
In collective crescendo, we align.

So let us rise, let us create,
In the tapestry woven, we shape our fate.
For in this journey, together we flow,
In the music of life, we grow and glow.

Resounding Hearts

In quiet whispers, dreams take flight,
Resounding hearts in the calm of night.
With every pulse, a tale unfolds,
A symphony of secrets, softly told.

Through shadows cast by fading stars,
We find our way, no matter the scars.
In harmony, we stand as one,
Embracing the journey, a race well run.

Like ripples in water, hopes cascade,
In this vibrant world, we are unafraid.
Together we sing, together we soar,
Resounding hearts, forevermore.

In every heartbeat, love ignites,
A dance of souls under celestial lights.
Through valleys low, and mountains high,
With resounding hearts, we learn to fly.

When thunder roars and storms may brew,
We find our strength, me and you.
Hand in hand, through thick and thin,
In the echo of love, we always win.

Notes of Solace

In the breeze, a gentle tune,
Notes of solace, morning's boon.
Each whisper floats on tender air,
A melody of hope, a silent prayer.

Through tangled woods where shadows play,
We find the light to guide our way.
With every note, the heartbeats blend,
In the chorus of life, we transcend.

When rainy days blur the horizon,
We gather strength as dawn arrives on.
In trembling voices, we find our song,
Notes of solace where we belong.

For every sorrow, there's a rhyme,
In the rhythm of love, there's no time.
We dance beneath the silver moon,
With notes of solace, our hearts attune.

Together we'll weave this symphony,
A tapestry of dreams, you and me.
With every pause that life may bring,
In notes of solace, our spirits sing.

Cadence of Care

In gentle hands, the moments dwell,
A cadence of care, a soothing spell.
Together we flourish, roots entwine,
In the garden of life, our hearts align.

Through laughter shared and tearful nights,
In each embrace, the world feels right.
A tender touch, a promise made,
In the cadence of care, no love will fade.

Let worries drift like autumn leaves,
In every heartbeat, the heart believes.
With kindness sown in every glance,
We write the story of our dance.

In bustling days and quiet hours,
With mindful words, we share our powers.
Each moment cherished, a work of art,
In the cadence of care, we never part.

So here we stand, side by side,
With open hearts, we don't need to hide.
For in this rhythm, love is rare,
We flourish together in the cadence of care.

Together We Rise

From stormy skies to sunlit days,
Together we rise in countless ways.
With every challenge, we find our might,
In the tapestry of dreams, we ignite.

In laughter shared and trials faced,
With open arms, no fear is traced.
Hand in hand, we reach for the skies,
Together we rise, our spirits fly.

Through thick and thin, we stand our ground,
In unity's embrace, strength is found.
With every heartbeat, our hopes entwine,
In the symphony of life, we shine.

Though paths may twist and winds may shift,
In each other's gaze, we find our gift.
With courage blooming, we will not fall,
Together we rise, we conquer all.

With dreams that soar and voices clear,
In this journey, we have no fear.
Through every sunset, we'll find the prize,
For in love's embrace, together we rise.

Harmonies of Hopes

In dawn's embrace, dreams take flight,
Whispers of light, hearts ignite.
Together we rise, shadows fade,
Woven in songs, hope is laid.

Through valleys deep, our voices soar,
Melodies rich, forevermore.
Each note a promise, bright and true,
Harmonies born, me and you.

As rivers flow, we find our way,
Guided by stars, night turns to day.
In laughter shared, our spirits bound,
Resounding joy in every sound.

With every beat, we dance as one,
Chasing the rays of the golden sun.
With courage found, we face the strife,
In harmonies, we find our life.

A symphony crafted in trust's warm glow,
Together we flourish, together we grow.
In hopeful tones, we stand side by side,
In the music of dreams, we forever abide.

Tuning into Trust

In gentle whispers, we find our way,
A bond that builds with each passing day.
Tuning our hearts to the same sweet song,
In the realm of trust, we both belong.

Like branches intertwined, strong and free,
Finding our strength in harmony.
Through every trial, we pledge our grace,
In moments of doubt, our love we embrace.

The notes may falter, the rhythm may change,
Yet within the dance, nothing feels strange.
For trust is the anchor, steadfast and true,
In every heartbeat, I believe in you.

Together we rise, like the morning sun,
With every challenge, two become one.
In the melody of life, so bright and bold,
Tuning into trust, a story unfolds.

With every breath, a promise made,
A symphony of faith will never fade.
In the silence shared, we still feel the spark,
Guided by trust, we illuminate the dark.

Unity in Upliftment

With hands entwined, we begin to rise,
Together we conquer, reach for the skies.
In every struggle, we find our grace,
United in purpose, we embrace this space.

A tapestry woven with threads of care,
Each voice distinct, yet beyond compare.
In chorus we grow, each heart a part,
Uplifted by love, igniting the art.

In laughter and tears, we share our fate,
In unity's warmth, we radiate.
Through storms that may come, we stand as one,
Together we flourish, our journey begun.

With every step, we honor the bond,
In gratitude's light, our fears gone beyond.
Upliftment is found in the hearts that believe,
In unity's strength, together we weave.

So let us rejoice in the light we share,
Each moment a gift, each breath a prayer.
With open arms, we embrace the light,
In unity's dance, our spirits take flight.

Mutual Embrace in Melody

In the stillness of night, our hearts collide,
Wrapped in the warmth, where love cannot hide.
Every note we share, a story awaits,
In mutual embrace, we open the gates.

With gentle whispers that weave through the air,
A symphony of souls, a bond rare and fair.
In the dance of our dreams, we find our way,
Together we sing, come what may.

As stars bear witness to our sacred vow,
In every heartbeat, we breathe in the now.
With arms wide open, we face the dawn,
In melody's grace, all fears are withdrawn.

Through valleys and peaks, together we soar,
Each harmony rich, a tale to explore.
In the beauty of moments, forever we stand,
Mutual embrace, hand in hand.

So let the music spread far and wide,
In the embrace of trust, we forever abide.
With every chord struck, our spirits entwined,
In melody's warmth, our hearts are aligned.

Cadences of Community

In the heart of the town, we gather near,
Voices blend like music we hold dear.
Hands are reaching, stories to share,
Together we rise, showing we care.

Laughter echoes under the bright sun,
Unity forms when we work as one.
Fridays bring colors, a vibrant parade,
In every gesture, connections are made.

Evening whispers call for a prize,
In the warmth of friendship, the spirit lies.
From child to elder, the tales unfold,
In every heartbeat, a legacy told.

Side by side, through thick and thin,
We dance through the storm, together we win.
With every challenge, our bonds will grow,
In the rhythm of life, we take our flow.

So let the world see what hope can bring,
In the pulse of the people, we bravely sing.
For in each cadence, we find our way,
In the arms of community, we choose to stay.

Soundtrack of Solidarity

In every heart beats a common refrain,
A song of strength through joy and pain.
Echoes of courage fill the air,
Together we stand, a vibrant affair.

With hands united, we build and strive,
In the melody of life, we truly thrive.
Voices harmonize through trials faced,
In the chorus of change, our hopes are placed.

Drums of persistence, a rhythm we share,
In the dance of unity, showing we care.
Step by step, on this journey we trod,
In the soundtrack of life, we honor the flawed.

Let the music of kindness lead the way,
Through darkest nights to brighter day.
Each note a promise, each beat a bond,
In the heart of solidarity, we respond.

So lift your voice, let the world now hear,
A symphony of hope, where love is dear.
Together we create, a melody bold,
In the soundtrack of life, our story is told.

Reflections of Resilience

In the mirror of life, shadows may cast,
Yet strength within shines, holding steadfast.
Each trial faced, a lesson we learn,
In resilience, our spirits forever burn.

Through storms that rage and winds that bite,
We rise from the ashes, igniting the light.
Stories of struggle etch deep in our soul,
In every setback, we find our whole.

Hope flickers brightly, a flame in the dark,
With every breath, igniting the spark.
In moments of doubt, we gather the might,
Reflecting our courage, taking to flight.

With heartbeats strong, we forge our own way,
In the face of adversity, we choose to stay.
Refrains of endurance echo through time,
In reflections of resilience, we find our rhyme.

So embrace the struggle, let it unfold,
For within our journey, a story is told.
In each rising dawn, we learn to survive,
In the art of resilience, we come alive.

Verses of Valued Voices

In the tapestry of life, threads intertwine,
Each voice a color, a story divine.
Together we weave in a chorus of sound,
In verses of value, our truths are found.

Every whisper holds weight, every shout has grace,
A mosaic of dreams in this sacred space.
From youth to elder, the wisdom we share,
In the echoes of history, we breathe the air.

Annotations of love, our battles, our peace,
In the garden of voices, our spirit won't cease.
With passion and purpose, we gather round,
In verses of love, our hopes are unbound.

So listen closely, hear the heart sing,
For each contributes to the joy we bring.
In diverse connections, our strength we unveil,
In valued voices, we will prevail.

Let the echoes resonate, carrying weight,
In the book of our lives, we craft our fate.
So lift your voice high, let the world rejoice,
In the power of many, we find our choice.

Strings of Solidarity

In the weave of shared dreams,
We find threads of hope and light.
Each heart beats with quiet strength,
Together we rise, hearts taking flight.

Chords of laughter echo wide,
In moments of joy, we unite.
With every hand that reaches out,
We create a tapestry bright.

Through storms that seek to divide,
Our bonds grow tighter each day.
Resilient, we stand side by side,
With love, we find our way.

In shadows, we share the weight,
Our voices merge in the dark.
With courage, we navigate fate,
Igniting hope's gentle spark.

These strings we hold, so intertwined,
Can weather every test we face.
In solidarity, we've designed,
A world filled with warmth and grace.

Frequencies of Friendship

In whispers shared beneath the stars,
We tune into each other's signs.
Each laugh a note that soars afar,
In harmony, our lives align.

Communicating heart to heart,
Through silence, we understand.
A melody that will not part,
In every touch, a gentle strand.

With every triumph, we rejoice,
In challenges, we lend our hands.
Through every silence, there's a voice,
That echoes through time's shifting sands.

Our laughter dances in the air,
A symphony of memories made.
Friendship's aura, ever rare,
A light that will never fade.

Together, we weave our dreams bright,
In every heartbeat, every glance.
Frequencies of love take flight,
In this beautiful, endless dance.

Harmonizing Our Voices

In unison, our voices rise,
A chorus echoing the night.
Each note a truth, a shared surprise,
Together, we create the light.

With every word, a story told,
Our hearts align in perfect tune.
A bond of warmth, fierce and bold,
Underneath the glowing moon.

Melodies that flow like streams,
Through valleys deep, across the plains.
In every harmony, there gleams,
The strength found in love's refrains.

Voices merge, creating peace,
In resolutions, we belong.
Through every strife, we find release,
United in a timeless song.

As we blend in perfect grace,
Together, we'll pave the way.
In every rhythm, every space,
Our voices lead, neither sway.

The Language of Lifting Up

In gentle words, we find our strength,
A language of support and care.
With every gesture, love's true length,
We rise together, hearts laid bare.

When shadows loom and spirits wane,
A smile can spark the darkest day.
Through kindness shared, we break the chain,
With every step, we light the way.

In every moment, great or small,
We lift each other, hand in hand.
The power of love conquers all,
A force that time cannot withstand.

With words of hope, we paint the skies,
Creating dreams where none exist.
In lifting up, our spirits rise,
In this sweet, unbreakable tryst.

Together, we forge a new dawn,
A tapestry of voices strong.
In unity, we will move on,
Creating a world where we belong.

Harmony in Helping Hands

In the shade of trees we stand,
Fingers entwined, hearts expand.
Together we lift, together we climb,
Crafting a world, one step at a time.

With each act of kindness, a bond is born,
In the face of struggle, compassion is sworn.
Voices united, we share the load,
Building a bridge along a shared road.

The rhythm of life in our gentle touch,
Every little effort, it matters so much.
In moments of need, we find our way,
Harmony glows when we choose to stay.

With warm smiles and laughter bright,
We weave together love and light.
In giving, we find joy that expands,
Painting the world with helping hands.

Together we rise, we bend, but don't break,
In every heartbeat, a promise we make.
When hands are joined, hope doesn't fade,
In the dance of life, our fears evade.

Echoes of Empathy

In the silence, a whisper flows,
Understanding blooms, and compassion grows.
Every story shared, a valued thread,
Woven together, where hearts are led.

Sunlight breaks through the shadows of doubt,
A touch, a glance, what life's about.
We carry each other, an unspoken pact,
In the depths of sorrow, we find the impact.

When voices tremble, we hold them near,
In echoes of solace, we conquer fear.
For every tear shed, a hand is reached,
In the warmth of embrace, a lesson is preached.

As raindrops fall and rivers sway,
Tides of emotions guide the way.
Through laughter and pain, we learn to see,
The echoes of empathy set our spirits free.

Together we rise, lifting the brave,
In the heart of the storm, we find the wave.
With every heartbeat, we dance through the night,
In echoes of empathy, we find our light.

Resonance of Resilience

When the world feels heavy, we stand tall,
With each setback we learn to enthrall.
Like trees in the storm, we sway yet remain,
Resilience within us, a bond we sustain.

In the heart of struggle, hope takes flight,
We gather our strength, ready to fight.
Through each trial, the spirit shines,
In the harshest times, true light aligns.

With every stumble, we gather our grace,
Learning that hardship is part of the race.
In the trenches of life, our courage unfolds,
Resonance of resilience, a story retold.

Join hands in the journey, side by side,
With every challenge, we'll turn the tide.
In the symphony of life's sweet refrain,
We rise from the ashes, again and again.

No mountain too high, no valley too low,
Together we flourish, together we grow.
In the cadence of hearts, our spirits align,
With resonance of resilience, our dreams intertwine.

Melodies of Mutual Aid

In every note, a story we share,
A symphony plays, with love in the air.
Through trials and triumphs, hand in hand,
Melodies soar, a united stand.

With every gesture, we brighten the room,
In acts of kindness, together we bloom.
From whispers of doubt to songs of delight,
In the harmony found, we ignite the night.

When shadows creep in, and hopes seem low,
We gather our voices, letting love flow.
The rhythm of aid, a pulse that connects,
In the chorus of life, our spirits reflect.

As melodies intertwine, we learn to embrace,
The beauty in giving, each moment we face.
In laughter and tears, our hearts intertwine,
With the melodies of mutual aid, we shine.

Through every challenge, a harmony grows,
With courage and compassion, our strength overflows.
In this grand composition, we find our song,
Together in unity, we'll always belong.

A Concert of Kindness

In a hall where hearts align,
Strings of love, they intertwine.
Gentle notes in soft embrace,
A melody of hope and grace.

Hands that reach across the isle,
Sharing warmth, a heartfelt smile.
In every word, a soothing balm,
A concert where we find our calm.

Voices rising, spirits soar,
Every kindness opens doors.
In this symphony we create,
A world reborn, it's not too late.

Harmony in every deed,
Planting love like a precious seed.
Together we can light the way,
In kindness, we shall choose to stay.

Final notes of sweet refrain,
Echoes linger, joy remains.
In unity, our hearts will sing,
A concert where all love takes wing.

The Pulse of Partnership

In every heartbeat, trust resides,
Together on this journey, side by side.
With shared dreams, we reach for stars,
Lighting the dark with hope, not scars.

Moments weave our stories tight,
Two spirits dance in shared delight.
When challenges arise, we stand,
Together strong, our hearts a band.

The rhythm flows, a bond unique,
In every silence, love can speak.
With open hearts, we find a tune,
In every dusk, we greet the moon.

Through trials faced, we learn and grow,
In partnership, the strength we show.
Together building, hand in hand,
In unity, we make our stand.

As seasons change, we hold the line,
In every moment, you are mine.
The pulse of partnership beats true,
With every step, I walk with you.

Interwoven Waves

On shores where dreams in silence wade,
Interwoven waves, life's serenade.
With every rush, new stories told,
In whispered breaths, adventures unfold.

The ebb and flow, a dance of grace,
Nature's rhythm, a warm embrace.
Boundless tides, a fearless crest,
In unity, we find our rest.

Moments surge like ocean's roar,
Together on this timeless shore.
In laughter shared, our spirits rise,
As seagulls dance beneath the skies.

Drifting freely, hand in hand,
Through every storm, here we stand.
Each wave a chance, each tide a gift,
In interwoven hearts, we lift.

As night falls and stars appear,
In starlit depths, we shed our fear.
With every wave, we dive anew,
In this vast ocean, just us two.

Orchestration of Hope

From shadows deep, a light will rise,
In every corner, love defies.
A symphony begins to play,
With every dawn, a brand new day.

In whispered dreams and gentle sighs,
Hope reawakens, never dies.
Each note a promise, bold and bright,
Guiding us through the darkest night.

Through every heart that dares to dream,
We weave a world, a hopeful gleam.
With every voice, we sing aloud,
In unity, we stand so proud.

The conductor leads with steady hand,
As melodies unite and expand.
In harmony, we find our place,
An orchestration, a sacred space.

Together we can shape the song,
In every heart, we all belong.
A world reborn, where love won't fade,
In orchestration, hope is made.

Lifelines in Lyrics

In whispers soft, a tale unfolds,
Emotions dance, like stories told.
Every note a heartbeat, true,
Binding souls in shades of blue.

Echoes linger in the night,
Songs of loss, and of delight.
Melodies that soothe the pain,
A refuge found in the refrain.

Chords that stretch across the years,
Healing wounds, dissolving fears.
In lyrics lost, we find our way,
Guiding hearts toward the day.

Each verse a lifeline, cast with care,
In harmony, we find our share.
Through music's thread, we weave and sew,
Connected always, come wind or snow.

As melodies entwine, we rise,
Finding hope in shared goodbyes.
Together in this vibrant sound,
In every note, our lives are found.

Overture of Occasion

Beneath the stars, a spark ignites,
Moments cherished, pure delights.
Celebrations, hand in hand,
A chorus strong, a joyful band.

With laughter bright, we greet the day,
In every heart, a grand ballet.
Life's sweet dance, a flowing stream,
We twirl and spin, lost in a dream.

A table set with love and grace,
Stories woven in each face.
Together we share, we reminisce,
In every hug, a moment's bliss.

To raise a glass, to toast the night,
Every glance reflects the light.
In unity, our spirits soar,
An overture we all adore.

As candles flicker, wishes made,
In this embrace, our fears do fade.
Cherish each moment, let it flow,
Life's grand party, let love grow.

Resounding Together

In harmony, our voices blend,
Every note, a heart to mend.
Resounding truths, a timeless song,
Together, we feel we belong.

Through valleys low and mountains high,
In every laugh and every sigh.
We lift each other, hand in hand,
Creating dreams where hope can stand.

A symphony of souls unite,
In shadows dim, we find the light.
With every chord and every verse,
Together, we rise to traverse.

In whispered prayers, our wishes soar,
Resounding love forever more.
Through trials faced, we find our way,
In this refrain, we choose to stay.

Together we sing through the night,
Every heartbeat shares the light.
In every echo, we find our song,
Resounding together, we are strong.

Threads of Togetherness

In woven ties, our souls connect,
Threads of love, we all select.
With every laugh and every tear,
Together stitched, we're always near.

A tapestry of dreams we weave,
Colors bright, they never leave.
Through trials faced, through joys and pain,
Together strong, we rise again.

In every heartbeat's gentle thrum,
The fabric of our lives becomes.
Each thread a story, intertwined,
In this embrace, our hearts aligned.

When shadows fall, we hold on tight,
Illuminated, our spirits bright.
In kindness shared, our hearts take flight,
Threads of togetherness ignite.

As dawn breaks forth, a brand new day,
In every moment, come what may.
United always, we'll face it all,
In threads of love, together we stand tall.

Shared Strength in Sound

In the hush of night, we gather near,
Voices blend softly, casting out fear.
Each note a promise, each chord a tie,
Together we rise, lifting hearts high.

Echoes of laughter fill the air,
Strong melodies weave through our shared care.
Hands gripping tightly, we face the dawn,
With every heartbeat, our hope is reborn.

Through trials we journey, hand in hand,
Finding our strength in the life we planned.
Every whisper shared, a bond made strong,
In shared sound, we find where we belong.

Together, we sing, our fears laid bare,
In the dance of life, we shall not despair.
With harmony flowing, let passions ignite,
Our voices united, a powerful sight.

So let the music guide our way,
In shared strength, may we forever stay.
With every song sung, we create our fate,
For in sound, my friend, love conquers hate.

The Rhythm of Relations

In every heartbeat, we find our pace,
Life's fleeting moments, we softly embrace.
Through laughter and tears, we dance in sync,
In the rhythm of relations, we link.

With every conversation, a story unfolds,
In the tapestry woven, our truth is told.
Like gentle waves lapping on the shore,
In the rhythm of relations, we explore.

Each smile exchanged, a soft serenade,
Together we navigate, never afraid.
As seasons change, our bonds remain tight,
In the rhythm of relations, we find light.

Through storms we weather, side by side,
Our hearts intertwined, in love we abide.
With compassion our guide, we'll rise from the night,
In the rhythm of relations, we're a beautiful sight.

And as we journey, may we always hold,
These moments of treasure, worth more than gold.
In the dance of our lives, let the music play,
For in rhythm, dear friend, love finds its way.

Interweaving Fates in Song

Beneath the stars, our paths collide,
Through melodies sweet, our souls abide.
Each note a whisper of fate's gentle hand,
Interweaving lives in this vast land.

As seasons shift, and time rolls on,
We weave a fabric, both fragile and strong.
From laughter to sorrow, we find our theme,
In the tapestry of life, we live the dream.

Voices harmonizing in the soft twilight,
Crafting our futures, embracing the night.
With every chorus, our spirits arise,
Interweaving fates under endless skies.

Through journeys unknown, we share our song,
In the threads of connection, we all belong.
With courage and love, we'll face the unknown,
In interwoven fates, we have grown.

So let the music play, let it unfold,
In every heartbeat, let stories be told.
For in the dance of life, we find our place,
Interweaving fates, in time's warm embrace.

Overture of Outreach

In the dawn of connection, we rise,
Hands reaching out, under vast skies.
Voices united, a harmonious call,
Together we stand, breaking down walls.

Each step we take, a bond we weave,
In every heart, the hope we believe.
Through laughter and tears, we find our way,
Embracing the journey, come what may.

From shadows of doubt, to brightened days,
We spark the light, ignite the rays.
With courage to share, and dreams to unfold,
The tales of our kindness, forever told.

The tapestry rich, with colors so bold,
Stories of strangers, now treasures to hold.
In compassion's embrace, we dare to explore,
For every connection opens the door.

Overture of outreach, our song takes flight,
In the rhythm of hearts, we shine so bright.
Joined in the dance, let our spirits soar,
Together we echo forevermore.

Prelude to Partnership

In the cradle of trust, we begin,
Crafting our dreams, where hope is keen.
Two paths converge, to form a new trail,
Strengthened by unity where others might fail.

With shared visions, we gather around,
In silence, we listen, our purpose profound.
Each voice a note, in the symphony played,
A melody forged, in efforts displayed.

Through challenges faced, we stand side by side,
Building a bridge where love will abide.
Together we rise, in each soaring stride,
With hearts intertwined, we take on the tide.

The laughter we share, a bond we find,
In moments of joy, our spirits aligned.
Each lesson a gift, each setback a guide,
In this prelude, our futures abide.

With visions so grand, we chart our course,
Embracing the journey, trusting the source.
In partnership bright, we shall ever stand,
With dreams intertwined, together we'll plan.

Collaborations in Chorus

Voices in harmony, ringing so clear,
Notes of togetherness, drawing us near.
In the chorus of hope, we stand hand in hand,
Crafting a future, united we'll stand.

Through verses of kindness, we sing our refrain,
In every endeavor, together we gain.
From whispers of doubt to crescendos of trust,
In collaborations sweet, it's love that we must.

As shadows may linger, our spirits unite,
With hearts all ablaze, we ignite the night.
Together we flourish, in talents combined,
In this grand tapestry, our dreams intertwined.

Each moment a treasure, a note in our song,
In the beauty of teamwork, we truly belong.
Through trials and triumphs, we celebrate all,
In collaborations, together we fall.

Let the music of friendship forever resound,
In the rhythm of service, our purpose profound.
In the chorus of life, we find our way,
With arms open wide, we embrace each day.

Flourishing in Fellowship

In gardens of fellowship, we find our roots,
Nurtured by kindness, where love distributes.
With every blossom, a story to tell,
In nurturing hands, together we dwell.

Through seasons of change, we rise and we grow,
In unity's glow, we steal the show.
With laughter like rain, and joy as the sun,
In the warmth of connection, we shine as one.

Each heartbeat a rhythm, a dance to be shared,
In fellowship's embrace, we show that we cared.
Through miles we traverse, through width and through height,
With dreams that we chase, we light up the night.

In circles of friendship, our spirits do soar,
In the love that we share, we're never unsure.
With hearts open wide, we gather anew,
Flourishing together, in all that we do.

With purpose aligned, our futures embrace,
In unison's strength, we find our safe space.
Together we flourish, this bond we will cherish,
In the garden of life, our love will not perish.

Sanctity of Support

In quiet storms, we stand so tall,
Bound by trust, we won't let fall.
Hands entwined in darkest night,
We shield each other, hearts ignite.

With every struggle, side by side,
In whispered hopes, we must confide.
The strength of love, a sacred rite,
Together we embrace the light.

In crowded rooms, we find our space,
Through every challenge, we embrace.
A promise made, to lift and guide,
In this journey, we bide our pride.

Through peaks and valleys, never alone,
In every heart, our seeds are sown.
With laughter shared, and tears that flow,
Our bond, the truth we always know.

So here we stand, in trust reborn,
A testament, through night and morn.
With every heartbeat, solid ground,
In sanctity of love, we're found.

Supportive Sojourn

We wander paths both tough and bright,
In every shadow, we find light.
Steps united, hearts aligned,
In every challenge, strength defined.

Through distant lands, our spirits soar,
With every laughter, we explore.
In moments shared, our journeys blend,
With every turn, a loyal friend.

When storms arise, we stand our ground,
With whispered hopes, our dreams abound.
From every fall, we rise anew,
In supportive arms, we push on through.

In times of doubt, we speak our truth,
With every shadow, we find proof.
Together facing winds that churn,
In this sojourn, our hearts will burn.

So hand in hand, we forge ahead,
With every word, our souls are fed.
In supportive grace, we shall believe,
With every step, we learn to weave.

Anthems of Affection

In every glance, a story shared,
In gentle smiles, we show we cared.
With every note, a song we sing,
Anthems of love that we will bring.

In days of joy, and nights of fear,
Through every laugh, we bring each cheer.
Our melodies, both soft and bold,
In every embrace, a love retold.

With whispered dreams beneath the stars,
Together, love eclipses scars.
We dance through storms, we glide on air,
In every heartbeat, love's our prayer.

The echoes swell, our voices rise,
In shared resolve, we touch the skies.
With every step, we write our fate,
In antiphonal hearts, we celebrate.

So let us sing this timeless song,
With arms wide open, where we belong.
In every note, we shall remain,
The anthems of affection, our refrain.

Resonating with Respect

In quiet moments, we embrace,
The strength of bond in every space.
With gentle words, our spirits rise,
Resonating with respect, so wise.

Through every trial, we find our way,
With open hearts, we choose to stay.
In every tear, a lesson learned,
With mutual trust, our souls are turned.

In every choice, we seek to share,
With kindness wrapped in tender care.
Through wrongs and rights, we navigate,
In shared wisdom, we appreciate.

The tapestry of life we weave,
In every thread, we shall believe.
With voices soft, yet firm and clear,
Resonating love, we hold near.

So hand in hand, we face the dawn,
With every sunrise, we press on.
In reverence to the paths we choose,
In respect and love, we never lose.

The Chorus of Care

In whispers soft, we gather near,
To share our joy, to calm our fear.
With open hearts, we weave our song,
In unity, we all belong.

The threads of kindness, brightly spun,
A tapestry where love has won.
Through trials faced, we stand as one,
Together always, never done.

In laughter shared, our spirits soar,
In moments cherished, we explore.
A chorus strong, our voices blend,
In harmony, our hearts will mend.

So heed the call, let not love fade,
In giving care, no debt is made.
With every note, a flame ignites,
A beacon bright, through darkest nights.

In shadows cast, we find our light,
In every heart, our hope ignites.
Bound by a purpose, so profound,
In every soul, our love is found.

Refuge in Rhythm

In every beat, we find our place,
A gentle pulse, a warm embrace.
With every step, we move as one,
A dance alive, a rising sun.

The music swells, a soothing balm,
In troubled times, we find our calm.
Through melody, our hearts unite,
In harmony, we shine so bright.

Each note a whisper of our dreams,
In every silence, hope redeems.
Together we sway, through highs and lows,
In rhythm's grace, our spirit grows.

In shared cadence, we find our strength,
With love as our guide, we go the length.
Through every storm, we'll dance and sing,
In the refuge of rhythm, joy takes wing.

So step in time, let worries cease,
In every movement, find your peace.
In unity, let the music play,
In refuge rich, we'll find our way.

Confluence of Connection

In rivers of trust, we intertwine,
Each heart a source that brightly shines.
With every wave, our spirits blend,
In this confluence, we ascend.

Through winding paths, we share our tales,
In every journey, love prevails.
With hands held high, we cross new plains,
In unity, we break the chains.

In laughter shared and tears released,
We find the strength when hope has ceased.
Through joyful songs and quiet sighs,
Our bond a treasure that never dies.

From diverse shores, we find our truth,
In honest words, we reclaim our youth.
Through every challenge, side by side,
In connection's strength, we can't divide.

So let us flow, let love enhance,
In this embrace, we find our chance.
Through every moment, let's reaffirm,
In this confluence, we will endure.

Symphony of Supportive Spirits

In melodies of hope, we find our way,
With every note, we seize the day.
Together we rise, through thick and thin,
In this symphony, we all begin.

In every chord, a story told,
Of love unyielding, strong and bold.
When trials loom and shadows clash,
Our harmonies unite, we'll make a splash.

With voices joined, we stand so tall,
In every echo, we hear the call.
Supportive spirits, hand in hand,
In this grand overture, we'll take a stand.

Through crescendos loud and soft refrains,
We find our peace amidst the strains.
In unity, our dreams take flight,
In the symphony, our hearts ignite.

So let the music fill the air,
In every moment, show we care.
In this creation, we'll leave our mark,
A symphony bright, igniting the spark.

Strings of Support

In the quiet night, we weave our dreams,
Stronger together, like tangled seams.
A gentle hand, a heart aligned,
In every silence, our love we find.

When shadows fall, we hold the light,
Guiding each other through darkest night.
Threads of compassion, woven tight,
A tapestry bright, in shared flight.

With every whisper, a bond we share,
In laughter and tears, we find our care.
Like strings of a harp, we resonate,
Creating sweet harmony, never too late.

In moments of doubt, we stand as one,
Bearing each other 'til the work is done.
In the fabric of life, our colors blend,
A beautiful story that will never end.

Together we rise, through thick and thin,
In the dance of life, we always win.
Strings of support, a precious thread,
In love's gentle embrace, we're always led.

Choir of Cherished Souls

In the still of dawn, our voices blend,
A choir of souls, where hearts transcend.
Each note a blessing, a shared refrain,
In perfect harmony, we ease the pain.

With laughter like bells, we fill the air,
In joy and sorrow, our hearts laid bare.
Every melody, a soft embrace,
In this sacred space, we find our place.

Through trials faced, we sing anew,
A symphony formed from me and you.
United in song, our spirits soar,
In the choir of life, forevermore.

Together we rise, like waves of sound,
Each voice uplifted, together we're found.
In chorus we stand, through storm and strife,
In the choir of cherished souls, we sing life.

As the stars appear, our voices light,
Guiding each other through the night.
In every heart, a song resides,
In this choir of love, the spirit abides.

The Song of Togetherness

In the dawn's embrace, we start each day,
Together we walk, come what may.
Hand in hand, hearts open wide,
In the song of togetherness, we're side by side.

Through laughter and tears, our spirits blend,
Every moment cherished, love we send.
With each gentle touch, our souls ignite,
In the rhythm of life, we find our light.

When storms arise, we face the rain,
In unity's strength, we bear the strain.
With every heartbeat, we beat as one,
In the song of togetherness, we've just begun.

In harmony's dance, our joys unfold,
Every story shared is a treasure of gold.
Through valleys low and mountains high,
The song of togetherness will never die.

As seasons change, our bond stays true,
In the chorus of love, I sing with you.
With every note, our spirits soar,
In the song of togetherness, forevermore.

Voices in the Void

In the quiet night, whispers take flight,
Voices in the void, searching for light.
Echoes of longing fill the air,
Carried on dreams, a silent prayer.

Through the darkness, we call out loud,
Yearning for comfort in the shrouded crowd.
Each sound a beacon, a glimmer of hope,
In the vast unknown, together we cope.

With heavy hearts, we seek to be found,
Voices in the void, a soft, sacred sound.
In the spaces between, we learn to feel,
Finding connection, our wounds we heal.

As shadows linger, we stand with grace,
In the faces we meet, we find our place.
Creating a symphony from whispers and sighs,
Voices in the void, reaching for skies.

In the tapestry of life, threads intertwine,
Together we flourish, your heartbeat and mine.
With every breath, we rise and rejoice,
In the harmony found in our shared voice.

Notes of Nurture

Gentle whispers in the night,
Softly guiding through the fright.
A tender heart with every beat,
Brings the warmth of life, so sweet.

In tiny hands, the world is held,
With dreams and hopes that are compelled.
Through laughter shared and tears we shed,
Our stories weave, our spirits fed.

A garden grows with every care,
Roots entwined in love we share.
From soil rich with lessons learned,
A nurturing flame forever burned.

In quiet moments, seeds are sown,
In silent vows, our love has grown.
With every note, our hearts align,
In this embrace, our souls entwine.

Rhythms of Reliability

A steady beat, a pulse so true,
With every step, I walk with you.
Through storms and sun, we find our way,
Together strong, come what may.

In laughter loud and whispered sighs,
A bond that never fades or dies.
With every promise softly made,
In trust we forge, our fears allayed.

The clock may tick, the seasons change,
Yet in our hearts, we remain.
For in the rhythms that we play,
Reliability will always stay.

Through trials faced and burdens shared,
In steadfast love, we're always bared.
With every moment, every glance,
We dance together, take a chance.

Ballad of Friendships

In twilight's glow, our laughter rings,
With memories made, the joy it brings.
Through ups and downs, we navigate,
   A friendship true, forever great.

With open hearts, we share our dreams,
In whispered thoughts and sunlit beams.
Through trials faced and skies so gray,
   A bond that holds, come what may.

The stories told, the tears we've shared,
   In every moment, love declared.
With every hug, a promise stays,
In this sweet song, friendship plays.

As seasons change, our roots grow deep,
In laughter's light, the memories keep.
Together, bold, we chase the light,
In every day, our hearts take flight.

Harmonies of Hope

In quiet dawn, the world awakes,
With whispered dreams and soft heartaches.
A melody of sweet resolve,
In hope, we find the problems solved.

With every note, the spirit soars,
Unlocking wide our hidden doors.
Through trials faced, we stand as one,
Beneath the light of the rising sun.

In darkest times, we lift our song,
Finding strength where we belong.
With hands entwined, we face the storm,
Creating light, embracing warm.

The stars above, they shine so bright,
Guiding us through the endless night.
In every heart, a spark ignites,
Harmonies of hope take flight.

Harmony in Togetherness

In the dance of life we sway,
Embracing each other's way.
A symphony built on trust,
In our hearts, a blend of rust.

Together we rise, not alone,
In our journeys, seeds are sown.
Vibrant voices, a single song,
In this bond, we all belong.

With every smile, we ignite,
Shining beams of purest light.
Hand in hand, we share the load,
Together we carve the road.

Through the storms, we'll hold tight,
Guided by love's brilliant light.
In every look, a thread of grace,
Harmony blooms in this space.

Let the world hear our refrain,
A tapestry woven from pain.
In the warmth of each embrace,
Harmony finds its sacred place.

Echoes of Encouragement

Whispers of hope fill the air,
Soft reminders that we care.
In moments dark, a light appears,
Echoes soothe away the fears.

Words like blossoms, gently spread,
Lifting spirits, where they're led.
A heartfelt cheer, a steady hand,
Together, we bravely stand.

Through the valleys, shadows cast,
We find strength, our voices vast.
In shared triumphs, nightly dreams,
We move onward, bursting seams.

With every challenge, we will rise,
In the laughter, in the cries.
A chorus builds, our hearts unite,
In echoes strong, we take flight.

Celebrate the path we roam,
For encouragement leads us home.
In this journey, side by side,
Our voices blend in joyous pride.

A Chorus of Compassion

In the silence, a heart's gentle plea,
Listen closely, and you might see.
A chorus swells, love's sweet refrain,
In compassion, we find our gain.

Every tear that falls, we share,
Threads of kindness fill the air.
With open arms, we hold the lost,
In this chorus, we pay the cost.

Together we weave a vibrant thread,
In love's garden, where hope is bred.
With every gesture, big or small,
Compassion's echo calls to all.

Through trials faced, we softly sing,
In unity, our voices ring.
With gentle hearts, we heal the pain,
A tapestry of joy remains.

As the world spins on its way,
In compassion, we'll brightly stay.
Together, a chorus we will raise,
In every heart, our song will blaze.

Melodies of Unity

In the rhythm of shared delight,
Melodies soar into the night.
With every note, we grow as one,
In unity, our song's begun.

Verse by verse, we shape our tale,
Together, we will never fail.
A harmony, strong and clear,
In every heartbeat, we draw near.

As the sun sets, we lift our hands,
In this circle, together stands.
With voices raised, we break the mold,
An orchestra in stories told.

Through every storm, the music plays,
In unity, our spirits blaze.
Weaving dreams in every land,
In this melody, we stand.

So let us sing in bright arrays,
A testament in all our days.
For in this sound, we find the key,
Melodies of unity set free.

Milton Keynes UK
Ingram Content Group UK Ltd.
UKHW020816141124
451205UK00012B/594